"This book is a voice that is calling you higher and a map to guide you to the sacred work of restoration"

Okwudili Iloka

RISE UP AND BUILD

My Time of Restoration

London, UK

RISE UP AND BUILD

My Time of Restoration

Stephen Irie – Oracle
2025
The Iries Publishing
www.stephenirie.com

RISE UP AND BUILD: My Time of Restoration
Copyright © 2025 by **Stephen Irie**.

All rights reserved, no part of this publication may be reproduced, stored in a retrieval system, or transmitted by any means without the written permission of the publisher and the author.

Unless otherwise indicated, all Scripture references in this book are from the King James Version 1769 Oxford Edition (KJV).

All extracts from the Authorized Version of the Bible (the King James Bible), the rights in which are vested in the Crown, are reproduced by permission of the Crown's Patentee, Cambridge University Press.

ISBN: 978-0-9575316-7-3

Published by
The Iries Publishing
stephenirie@hotmail.com,
+44 (0)7925525434

OracleIrie @ Facebook/ Meta, Instagram, X, TikTok…
www.stephenirie.com

For Purchase
This book is available for purchase from Amazon,
for bulk purchase contact us. stephenirie@hotmail.com
+44 (0)7925525434

Contents

Dedication vii
Foreword ix
Preface xi
Introduction xiii
Chapter I   **Making Inventory** 17
Chapter II   **Make the Right Decisions** 27
Chapter III   **Getting To Work** 39
   a.   Overcoming Procrastination 40
   b.   The Power of Community 43
   c.   Overcoming Opposition 45
   d.   Seeing the Project Through 46
Chapter IV   **Watch Out For Enemies** 49
   a.   External Enemies 51
   b.   Internal Enemies 53
   c.   Kick out your Jonah 57
Chapter V   **Building Momentum** 63
   a.   Strong Foundation 64
   b.   Taking Consistent Action 67

c.	Overcoming Setbacks	69

Chapter VI **The Final Touches** 71

    a. Attention to Detail 73

    b. Adding the Finishing Touches 75

    c. Spiritual Refinement 76

Chapter VII **Faithful Finishing** 81

Chapter VIII **Celebration** 87

    a. Understanding your True Identity 96

    b. Living in your Identity 98

    c. Walking in your Victory 99

    d. A New Mindset for Dedication 100

Bibliography 103

About The Author 105

About The Publisher 107

Dedication

To my beloved wife, Lois,

Your love, unwavering support, and endless encouragement have been my greatest source of strength. You are my partner, my confidante, and the light that guides me through every challenge. This book is as much a reflection of your grace and inspiration as it is of my journey.

Thank you for walking with me every step of the way, for believing in me when I doubted, and for always lifting me up with your love. May this book be a testament to the power of restoration and the beauty of walking in purpose, just as we have together, in the name of Jesus.

With all my love,

Stephen

Main Scriptures

Then I told them of the hand of my God which was good upon me; as also the king's words that he had spoken unto me. And they said, Let us rise up and build. So they strengthened their hands for this good work.
Neh.2:18

The LORD says, "I will give you back what you lost to the swarming locusts, the hopping locusts, the stripping locusts, and the cutting locusts…
Joel 2:25

Foreword

In life, we often find ourselves standing amidst the ruins of shattered dreams, unfulfilled hopes, and the remnants of battles we thought we had conquered. Yet, it is within these moments of brokenness that the divine call to restoration echoes the loudest. Bishop Stephen Irie's Rise Up and Build: My Time of Restoration is not just a book; it is an invitation—a profound summons to rise, rebuild, and reclaim the beauty of what has been lost.

Inspired by the timeless story of Nehemiah, this work transcends a simple recounting of biblical events. It is a guide, filled with practical wisdom and spiritual insight, that equips us to navigate the complexities of our individual journeys. It reminds us that restoration is not merely about the physical rebuilding of walls or the recovery of possessions; it is about renewing purpose, reawakening faith, and aligning ourselves with the divine plan woven into the fabric of our existence.

The process of restoration requires courage—courage to assess the ruins, confront the challenges, and trust the divine hand that promises to guide us through. Bishop Stephen masterfully blends scriptural truths with practical applications, offering a blueprint for those ready to embrace the work of restoration. From making inventory of our lives to overcoming opposition, this book speaks to the heart of anyone longing to rebuild—whether spiritually, emotionally, or physically.

In a world that often measures success by how much we accumulate or how seamlessly we appear to have it all together, this book reminds us that restoration is about wholeness, not perfection. It is about allowing the divine presence within us to illuminate the path forward, transforming setbacks into stepping stones and pain into purpose.

As you turn these pages, you will find more than words; you will discover a spirit of encouragement, a voice that calls you higher, and a map that guides you to the sacred work of restoration. Whether you are rebuilding relationships, rediscovering your faith, or simply seeking clarity in the midst of life's noise, this book offers timeless principles grounded in eternal truths.

Let Rise Up and Build: My Time of Restoration awaken within you the boldness to rise, the faith to believe, and the resolve to build. God promises restoration for all who are willing to trust the process and take the first step. May this book inspire you to step into your own season of renewal and transformation.

With Love, Gratitude and Expectation.

Okwudili Iloka
Author of Dear Christian: A Letter From Christ, Good is God and From Poverty to Power

Preface

As I reflect on the journey that led me to write *RISE UP AND BUILD: My Time of Restoration*, I realize that this book is more than just a reflection of my experiences—it is a call to action. A call to those who are tired, those who have lost hope, those who are at the brink of giving up, those who feel broken, and those who have allowed the setbacks of life to define them. In the story of Nehemiah, we see a man who, despite the devastation around him, decided to take bold steps to restore what had been lost. His journey was not easy, but it was purposeful, and it was grounded in faith.

This book is my own personal testament to that same spirit of restoration. When I found myself in a season of hopelessness and brokenness—whether emotionally, physically, spiritually, financially or in my relationships—I turned to Nehemiah's example and realized that, like him, I had the power to rebuild. I can get back on my feet. Through prayer, reflection, decision and action, I embarked on a year-long journey of restoration. In these pages, I share the lessons I learned along the way, the challenges I faced, and the victories I celebrated.

You will come out of that situation, it is not permanent, trust the process, God is in the driving seat.

Each chapter serves as a guide for anyone who feels called to rebuild the walls in their own life—whether that means restoring their health, mending relationships, or rekindling their faith. My hope is that through this book, you will find the inspiration, tools, and encouragement you need to rise up, rebuild, and step into the life you are meant to live. This is not just a book about restoration; it's a book about transformation, a blueprint for rebuilding your life, piece by piece, with God's help.

May this book inspire you to take the first step toward your own restoration, knowing that no matter how broken things may seem, God's promise is to restore, heal, and rebuild.

When it comes to restoration, I can boldly say
'I am a living testimony.'
Stephen Irie - Oracle

Introduction

A Call to Restoration.

Every new day, new week, new month or new year brings with it the promise of new beginnings. It's a fresh start, a blank canvas on which to paint our dreams, hopes, and plans. Yet, as we step into this new chapter, it's easy to feel weighed down by the remnants of the past — unfinished goals, broken relationships, unfulfilled promises, and perhaps even a sense of spiritual or emotional depletion. This is where the idea of restoration becomes crucial. What does it mean to restore? To bring back to a former, better state. Restoration involves renewal, rebuilding, and rejuvenation, but more importantly, it requires action. It's about taking the necessary steps to bring something back to its fullest potential.

In the Bible, we are presented with the story of Nehemiah, to which I have been exposed in 1999 during the mega crusade of prophet Kacou Severin from Ivory Coast in London (intitled LET US RISE AND BUILD). Nehemiah was a man of vision and determination who was called to rebuild the walls of Jerusalem, which had been destroyed and left in ruins.

Nehemiah's journey was not just about physical reconstruction but also about restoration of hope, identity, and purpose for the people of Israel. His story, found in the Old Testament, is one of resilience in the face of opposition, a steadfast commitment to the task at hand, and an unshakable faith in God's promises.

As we reflect on Nehemiah's journey, we see a man who took inventory of the situation, made bold decisions, got to work, and overcame both external and internal enemies—all while keeping his eyes on the prize. His story is one of complete restoration: not just of the walls of a city, but of the community and the people's relationship with God. Joel 2:25 further reinforces this idea of restoration: "I will restore to you the years that the swarming locust has eaten..." This verse speaks of God's faithfulness to restore what has been lost, destroyed, or taken away, and it is this promise that serves as the foundation for this book. In the same way that Nehemiah rose up to rebuild the walls of Jerusalem, we are called to rise up and rebuild the aspects of our own lives that have fallen into ruin. Whether it's our spiritual walk, our relationships, our careers, or even our sense of self-worth, there is a rebuilding to be done. This year, this month, this season can be your moment of restoration—a time to take stock of what has been lost or broken and actively work toward restoring it.

My personal journey of restoration began during a profound season of reflection—a time when I was forced to confront the realities of my life and the broken pieces it had become. I had reached a point where it felt like too many things had gone wrong, and I was left questioning how it all unraveled.

Some of my dreams, once vivid and full of promise, remained unfulfilled. The churches I had passionately established on an international scale, with a vision to transform lives and spread hope, were taken over by the very people I had trusted. Betrayal struck deep, and the relationships I once cherished had grown distant and fractured. The passion that had once been the heartbeat of my purpose seemed to fade, leaving behind a void that felt impossible to fill.

I was overwhelmed by a crushing sense of devastation, as though I had stumbled into an endless wilderness with no clear direction and no one to turn to for support. The weight of my losses was compounded by unjust accusations from close relatives. This were claims I had no connection to, designed solely to tarnish my reputation and erode the legacy I had worked so hard to build—BUT GOD IS GOD and has always been, Glory!

It was in this bleak and desolate season, when I had lost everything and was stripped of the confidence and security I once held, that my journey toward restoration began. It was a journey born out of necessity, a desperate cry for healing, renewal, and a way to rebuild from the ashes of my past. Little did I know, this wilderness was not my end but a catalyst for transformation—a place where God would begin to work in ways I could not yet comprehend.

There were moments when I felt exhausted by the magnitude of what needed fixing. Yet, as I sat down to evaluate my life, I realized that the key to moving forward wasn't to dwell on what had been lost, but to focus on what could be restored. That was the click. Just as Nehemiah took the time to survey the walls of Jerusalem and assess the damage, I too had to take inventory of my own life.

This year, I invite you to embark on your own journey of restoration. Like Nehemiah, you will face challenges, but you will also experience moments of triumph. You will face opposition from external and internal forces—people who question your vision or circumstances that seem to conspire against you. But, just as Nehemiah was able to rebuild the walls in 52 days despite all odds, you too can rebuild what has been lost in your life. The key is to stay focused, take action, and trust in God's promise of restoration. By the end of this year, I hope that you will not only have made significant strides in your personal restoration but also feel a deep sense of fulfillment and purpose.

So, as we begin this year, this season or this month, let us rise up and build. The walls may seem crumbled, and the road ahead may seem long, but as we take each step with faith, diligence, and courage, we will see the walls of our lives being restored. This is the moment of restoration. Let us walk boldly into it, knowing that God is with us every step of the way. Even if you are already halfway through the year, the season or the month, you still can set yourself up for restoration by the end of the period, by using and applying the principles highlighted in this book.

Enjoy your reading!

Chapter I

Making Inventory

Assessing the Ruins.

B efore Nehemiah began the monumental task of rebuilding the walls of Jerusalem, he took the time to carefully survey the situation, assessing the ruins and understanding the full scope of what needed to be done. In Nehemiah 2:11-17, we see Nehemiah arriving in Jerusalem, under the cover of night, and surveying the broken walls and burned gates that lay before him.

He did not rush into action without first taking inventory of the destruction; instead, he examined the situation with patience, wisdom, and a discerning heart. Only once he fully understood the scale of the task did he gather the people and begin the work of restoration.

This process of making inventory is crucial in any restoration journey. Before we can rebuild, we must first understand what has been lost or broken. This is not always an easy task, as it requires facing some uncomfortable truths about ourselves, our relationships, our finances, or our dreams. Just as Nehemiah had to walk through the ruins of Jerusalem to fully grasp the extent of the damage, we must also confront the areas of our lives that need healing, renewal, and rebuilding.

In my own life, making inventory was an eye-opening experience. Like many people, I had encountered setbacks, disappointments, and losses that had left me feeling disillusioned and uncertain about the future. But before I could begin the work of restoration, I had to take a hard look at where I was and identify the areas that

Making Inventory

needed the most attention. I began by examining my relationships—both the ones that had become strained and the ones I had neglected. I realized that I was all alone and there was no one to lean on. Something was missing. I needed a partner who will fall in line with my dreams and vision.

Over the years, I came to a sobering realization: I had allowed the busyness of life and countless distractions to pull me away from my primary goals. The demands of daily life—while necessary—had taken precedence over the deeper aspirations and dreams that once burned brightly within me. Somewhere along the way, I had permitted these dreams to fade into the background, overshadowed by the immediate concerns of the present.

This self-awareness led me to another, perhaps more significant, acknowledgment: for the past twenty years, I had been in the wrong environment. I had surrounded myself with the wrong people—individuals who, whether intentionally or not, contributed to the stagnation of my growth and the erosion of my focus.

Instead of fostering an atmosphere of encouragement, accountability, and inspiration, my surroundings had often hindered my ability to reach my fullest potential.

This recognition was both humbling and empowering. Humbling because it required me to admit where I had fallen short; empowering because it gave me the clarity I needed to realign my priorities, assess my environment, and make the necessary changes to rediscover my path. It was a call to action, a moment to rise above complacency and actively pursue the restoration of purpose in my life.

Let this serve as a reminder: the environment we choose and the people we surround ourselves with can significantly influence the trajectory of our lives. It is never too late to evaluate, to reset, and to commit to the journey of reclaiming the dreams and goals that truly matter.

Taking inventory also meant looking at my spiritual life. I had once been deeply passionate about my faith, but over time, as I was going through family breaking down and loss of hope, I had allowed complacency to creep in. My connection with God had become routine, and I no longer felt the same fire and excitement that I had once experienced. I knew that in order to restore my life, I had to first restore my relationship with God and seek His guidance for what needed to be rebuilt.

As difficult as it was, this process of assessment was absolutely necessary. It required honesty and vulnerability, but it also provided clarity. When Nehemiah surveyed the walls of Jerusalem, he did not sugarcoat the situation; he acknowledged the reality of the destruction. Similarly, we must be willing to face the truth about our lives, no matter how painful or uncomfortable it may be.

Only then can we begin to take the necessary steps to rebuild. One of the key aspects of making inventory is identifying the areas of our lives that have been neglected or damaged.

These may not always be immediately obvious, especially when life's distractions and pressures have caused us to overlook certain aspects of our well-being. We may not realize how much we have neglected our health, our finances, or our spiritual life until we take a step back and honestly assess where we are.

In my case, one of the most glaring areas of neglect was my well-being. For years, I had been so focused on work and other responsibilities that I had allowed my well-being to slip. I wasn't exercising regularly, and my eating habits had become unhealthy.

As I made inventory of my life, it became clear that my physical well-being was an area that needed immediate attention. I made the decision to prioritize my health in the same way I was focusing on rebuilding my relationships and spiritual life.

In addition to well-being, I also had to evaluate my financial situation. At the time, I had allowed certain financial habits to go unchecked — spending impulsively and failing to save for the future. While this wasn't something I liked to admit to myself, taking inventory meant acknowledging these areas where I had been irresponsible.

It also meant identifying where I had been successful, such as paying off debt or creating a small savings buffer, and building on those strengths.

Taking inventory is not just about identifying what's broken or missing; it's also about recognizing what remains. When Nehemiah arrived in Jerusalem and assessed the state of the city, he didn't just focus on the walls and gates that had been destroyed. He also recognized the importance of the resources and people available to him. He saw the potential in the people who were still living in the city, and he was able to rally them to the cause of rebuilding.

Similarly, when we assess our own lives, it's important to acknowledge the strengths, resources, and relationships we still have—things that can serve as the foundation for our restoration. During my own journey of inventory, I was surprised by the resources that were still available to me.

Despite many things in my life falling apart, I came to recognize that not everything was lost. Certain aspects of my life remained intact—most notably, my faith and my capacity to learn and grow. These resources became the foundation upon which I could begin rebuilding, providing me with the stability and resilience needed to take the next steps toward restoration.

To further solidify this foundation, I met my wife, Lois, who has been an incredible source of strength and unwavering support. Her presence and partnership have been instrumental in my journey, offering encouragement and companionship during moments when hope seemed distant.

Recognizing what was still in place—both within myself and in the relationships around me—gave me renewed motivation and a sense of purpose.

It reminded me that restoration does not begin with what has been lost, but with what remains. This realization fueled my determination to rebuild, knowing that even in the face of setbacks, there is always a foundation upon which a new and stronger future can be built.

One of the most important parts of making inventory is setting aside time for reflection and prayer. Nehemiah spent time in prayer before taking action, asking God for guidance and favor (Nehemiah 1:4-11). Similarly, taking inventory in our own lives should involve seeking God's wisdom. He is the ultimate restorer, and His guidance can help us identify the areas that need the most attention and give us the strength to take action. Prayer is not just a way to ask for help, but also a way to hear from God and receive His direction.

As you begin your own journey of restoration, I encourage you to take the time to assess your life honestly and thoroughly. Reflect on the relationships, goals, and areas of your life that need healing, and make a list of what needs to be rebuilt. Identify the resources and strengths you still have, and remember that God is with you in this process.

Just as Nehemiah did, you must take a moment to assess the situation before taking the next steps.

It may not be easy, but this step is essential for laying a solid foundation for the work ahead. Restoration, whether in our personal lives, relationships, or faith, begins with a moment of honest self-assessment. It is a process that requires humility, courage, and a willingness to confront the areas that have been neglected, broken, or torn down over time. Without this crucial step of taking inventory, any attempt to rebuild risks being built on shaky ground.

Before we can move forward, however, we must first pause. We must look closely at our own lives and honestly evaluate what needs to be restored. What have we lost along the way? What dreams have been abandoned, relationships strained, or habits formed that hinder progress? Just as Nehemiah began his mission by carefully assessing the broken walls of Jerusalem, we too must take inventory of our own lives. This process may uncover painful truths, but it is only by identifying the damage that we can begin to address it.

This initial step sets the stage for the transformative journey ahead. By taking stock of what needs restoration, we position ourselves to approach the work with clarity, purpose, and determination. It is the foundation upon which everything else will be built—a foundation that ensures we are not simply patching up cracks but rebuilding something strong, lasting, and meaningful.

As we move forward together, drawing inspiration from Nehemiah's example, let us embrace this moment of reflection with open hearts and minds. The path may be challenging, but it is one of hope and renewal. When we take inventory of our lives and prepare to address what has been broken, we align ourselves with the promise of restoration. And once we do, we will be ready—ready to rise up and build.

Indeed! **You are not just anybody.** You are chosen, set apart, and destined for greatness by the hand of God. **It is not over until God says so.** When the world tells you it's too late, when circumstances seem against you, or when others count you out—remember that God's final word is the only one that matters. He is the Alpha and the Omega, the Beginning and the End (Revelation 22:13). If God has spoken life, restoration, and victory over you, no obstacle can cancel His plan.

"What, then, shall we say in response to these things? If God is for us, who can be against us?" (Romans 8:31, NIV)

Your setbacks are not the end of the story. Joseph was thrown into a pit, imprisoned, and forgotten, but when God's time of favor came, he rose to power and fulfilled his destiny. Job lost everything, but when God spoke restoration, he received back double what he had lost. God specializes in turning mourning into joy, ashes into beauty, and hopeless situations into testimonies of His glory.

Keep building, keep trusting, and keep walking in faith. **When God declares "It is finished," that's when the story closes—not before.** Until then, hold on, because your breakthrough could be one step of faith away. What looks like the end to man is often the beginning of something greater with God.

Chapter II

Make the Right Decisions

Planning to Rebuild.

The process of restoration does not unfold by accident; it requires deliberate, well-informed decisions that set the course for rebuilding. In the story of Nehemiah, we see how crucial decision-making was in laying the foundation for the monumental task of restoring Jerusalem's walls.

After assessing the damage (Nehemiah 2:11-16), Nehemiah had to decide how, when, and with whose help he would undertake this rebuilding project. His success was not just a matter of divine favor, though that was certainly the greater factor; it was also the result of wise planning and strategic choices.

"Then the king said to me, 'What are you requesting?' So I prayed to the God of heaven. And I said to the king... 'send me to Judah... that I may rebuild it.'" (Nehemiah 2:4-5, ESV)

This brief exchange captures the heart of Nehemiah's decision-making process. He prayed, he acted, and he communicated clearly. The same holds true for our own journeys of restoration: we must acknowledge our dependence on God, then courageously move forward in faith, making decisions that align with our ultimate goals.

Joel 2:25 reminds us that God longs to restore the years that have been devoured. Yet for that restoration to manifest, we must partner with Him by making choices that usher in healing and renewal.

Prayerful Decision-Making

One of the most striking aspects of Nehemiah's story is how he saturated every major decision with prayer. In **Nehemiah 1:4-11**, we see him weeping and mourning for days, fasting and praying before the God of heaven. When the opportunity arose to speak with the king (Nehemiah 2:4), he offered up a quick, heartfelt prayer before presenting his request.

1. **Prayer Aligns Our Will with God's Will**
   It's easy to make decisions based on personal desires or external pressures. Prayer helps us align our intentions with God's higher purpose. By seeking His guidance, we position ourselves to receive divine wisdom that surpasses human logic.

2. **Prayer Instills Confidence and Peace**
   When we commit our decisions to God, we experience a peace that transcends circumstances (Philippians 4:6-7). Nehemiah approached the king with boldness because he knew his cause was anchored in prayer.

3. **Prayer Opens Doors**
   Nehemiah's prayerful approach paved the way for favor. Despite being a cupbearer — an unlikely candidate to rebuild a city — he received letters of safe passage and the resources needed to start the work (Nehemiah 2:7-8).

In my own life, I have seen how prayer can transform decision-making. On one occasion, I was at a crossroads about whether to remain in a comfortable job or step out in faith to pursue a more challenging role that aligned better with my long-term vision. Like Nehemiah, I spent days praying, journaling, and seeking wise counsel. When I finally made my decision, the confirmation and peace I felt made it clear that I was on the right path.

Counting the Cost

Setting Clear Goals and Boundaries

Once Nehemiah received the king's permission, he needed a plan. He surveyed the walls, counted the cost, and envisioned the resources and manpower required.

Effective decision-making involves looking at the bigger picture, understanding the potential risks and rewards, and making informed plans.

Jesus emphasized this principle in Luke 14:28 when He asked, "Which of you, wishing to build a tower, does not first sit down and count the cost...?"

Below are some practical points for making informed decisions:

- **Identify Clear Goals**
  Be precise about what needs to be rebuilt. Whether it's your finances, health, relationships, or spiritual life, clarity will help you stay focused.
  Example: "I need to restore my financial stability by creating and sticking to a budget within the next six months."

- **Evaluate Resources**
  Determine what you have and what you need. This could include time, money, relationships, or specific skills.
  Example: "I have an extra hour each morning I could use for self-improvement, and I have supportive friends who can mentor me in areas where I'm weak."

- **Anticipate Challenges**
  Be realistic about obstacles, both external and internal. Nehemiah had to plan for opposition from local governors and the sheer scale of the broken walls.
  Example: "I know I struggle with procrastination, so I'll set smaller milestones to keep myself accountable."

- **Establish Boundaries**
  Nehemiah's letters from the king protected him from interference (Nehemiah 2:7-9). In our own lives, setting healthy boundaries is vital to safeguarding our priorities.

Example: "I will turn off my phone during family time so I can rebuild my relationships without distractions."

By systematically addressing these points, you create a roadmap for success. Making the right decisions becomes more manageable when you have a clear set of goals, an understanding of your resources, and a plan to tackle challenges.

Seeking Wise Counsel

Proverbs 15:22 reminds us that "Without counsel plans fail, but with many advisers they succeed." Even though Nehemiah was a man of prayer and confidence, he did not rebuild Jerusalem's walls by himself. He relied on the wisdom and labor of others.

Part of making the right decisions is surrounding yourself with people who can offer honest feedback, share insights, and even challenge your assumptions.

- **Mentors and Spiritual Leaders**: These individuals can offer guidance based on their experiences and spiritual discernment.

- **Peers on a Similar Journey**: People who are walking similar paths can provide camaraderie and mutual support.

- **Professional Advisors**: Financial planners, counselors, or coaches may offer specialized knowledge.

In my own experience, I initially hesitated to ask for counsel, fearing it would expose my weaknesses. But once I humbled myself and reached out, I realized how empowering it was to share my vision with trusted friends, mentors and ministry colleagues.

They pointed out blind spots I never would have noticed on my own and helped me solidify my plans. In doing so, they became partners in my restoration process, much like the willing laborers who joined Nehemiah. I am forever grateful to them.

Balancing Faith and Action

Nehemiah's story is a masterclass in striking the balance between trusting God and taking personal responsibility. After praying and receiving favor, he actively organized the laborers, assigned specific sections of the wall to various families, and even implemented guard rotations when threats arose (Nehemiah 4:16-18). Faith does not negate the need for practical steps; rather, it undergirds them with divine strength.

"Commit your work to the Lord, and your plans will be established." (Proverbs 16:3, ESV)

- **Faith**: Believing that God will guide and sustain your efforts.

- **Action**: Doing your part diligently — planning, working, adjusting as needed.

When I was planning to restore a fractured relationship in our church, I prayed consistently for reconciliation. However, I also told the couple to take intentional steps like writing messages, setting up neutral meeting places for open conversations, and even seeking professional counseling in certain areas to navigate old wounds. It was a combination of spiritual reliance and concrete action that made the restoration possible.

Maintaining Perspective

Why Are You Rebuilding?

In the busyness of decision-making and planning, it's easy to lose sight of the greater vision.

Nehemiah's ultimate goal was not just to construct physical walls but to restore the dignity and identity of his people. Similarly, Joel 2:25 reminds us that God desires to restore what has been lost, not merely for our comfort but for His glory and our growth.

Ask yourself:

1. **What is My Motivation?**
   Is it to glorify God and serve others, or is it solely for personal gain?

2. **How Does This Align with My Values?**
   Are my decisions consistent with the principles of integrity, compassion, and stewardship?

3. **Who Will Benefit from This Restoration?**
   How can my rebuilding process help not just myself but also my family, community, or church?

By consistently revisiting the **"why,"** you keep your decisions anchored in purpose and avoid distractions that can derail your progress.

Personal Reflection

Looking back on my journey, I see pivotal moments where a single decision changed the trajectory of my life.

One such moment was choosing to leave a toxic environment that was draining my spiritual and emotional well-being. I wrestled with the fear of the unknown, the opinions of others, and the financial implications.

Yet, after seeking God in prayer, seeking wise counsel, and carefully counting the cost, I took the leap of faith.

It was not easy, but the outcome was a fresh start—a new environment where I could flourish and focus on restoring other broken areas in my life.

Practical Steps

In summary, consider these actionable points as you plan your own rebuilding:

- **Pray First and Continually**
  Like Nehemiah, never underestimate the power of a quick, heartfelt prayer at critical moments.

- **Count the Cost**
  Evaluate the resources required—time, money, energy—and plan accordingly.

- **Seek Wise Counsel**
  Involve mentors, friends, and professionals who can offer perspective and support.

- **Act in Faith**
  Trust God to make a way, but also take practical steps toward your goals.

- **Stay Flexible**
  Be prepared to adapt your plans as challenges or new insights emerge.

- **Revisit Your 'Why'**
  Keep your motivation front and center to maintain clarity and determination.

The decisions you make today form the foundation of your tomorrow. As Nehemiah shows us, prayerful, purposeful decisions pave the way for remarkable transformation. There will be obstacles, yet when you align your plans with God's will and commit them to His care, you step into the promise of restoration He so eagerly wants to bestow.

Remember Joel 2:25 — God is in the business of restoring lost years, but He often waits for us to invite His guidance into our planning. Making the right decisions is not merely an intellectual exercise; it is a spiritual, emotional, and practical pursuit that requires courage, humility, and tenacity. Turn to God in prayer, count the cost, mobilize your resources, and step out in faith. You are on the cusp of something extraordinary — the chance to see broken walls rebuilt, shattered dreams awakened, and lost hope restored.

As you stand on the threshold of your own rebuilding project, take a page from Nehemiah's story and recognize that every great work begins with faith, vision, and action. Nehemiah didn't just see the broken walls of Jerusalem as an insurmountable problem; he saw an opportunity for restoration through God's guidance. He fasted, prayed, and sought God's wisdom, understanding that spiritual preparation is just as important as physical action.

"The God of heaven will give us success. We his servants will start rebuilding." (Nehemiah 2:20, NIV)

Similarly, as you embark on rebuilding your life, your dreams, or your faith, approach the process with intentionality. Start with a clear vision of what restoration looks like for you. Identify what needs rebuilding—whether it's your spiritual life, relationships, health, or finances—and commit those areas to God in prayer. Like Nehemiah, seek wisdom, guidance, and strength from God before taking any step.

But don't stop at prayer; be prepared to act. Nehemiah rallied others to join him in the work, emphasizing unity and shared purpose. You don't have to rebuild alone. Surround yourself with people who can support you, hold you accountable, and help you stay the course. There will be obstacles, just as Nehemiah faced opposition from those who mocked and threatened the project. Yet, he didn't let fear dictate his actions.

Take courage as you rise to rebuild. Remember that what you are constructing is not just for today—it is a legacy of faith, resilience, and purpose that will endure. Just as Nehemiah completed the walls of Jerusalem through perseverance, prayer, and action, you too can see the fulfillment of your restoration. **Trust that God, who has begun this work in you, will bring it to completion.**

Chapter III

Getting To Work

The Act of Rebuilding.

Once Nehemiah had surveyed the ruins, made the necessary decisions, and received the king's blessing, the most important step came—he began to rebuild. In Nehemiah 3, we see that he didn't hesitate.

He mobilized the people, assigned specific sections of the wall to various families, and set them to work. This chapter of Nehemiah's story shows us that planning, although essential, is useless without action.

Restoration, whether in our personal lives, relationships, or careers, requires hard work, commitment, and the ability to persevere despite challenges.

"So we built the wall. And all the wall was joined together to half its height, for the people had a mind to work." (Nehemiah 4:6, ESV)

The phrase "the people had a mind to work" reveals a profound truth: restoration begins when we set our minds to action. It's not enough to desire change or envision a better future—we must commit to doing the work. This chapter will explore how to transition from planning and praying into practical, effective action that leads to rebuilding, healing, and growth.

a. Overcoming Procrastination

The Importance of Starting

Starting a project, especially one as significant as personal restoration, can be daunting.

The dream of what you hope to rebuild may seem so large, so far away, that it feels impossible to begin. Nehemiah faced a similar challenge — he was tasked with rebuilding a city's walls that had been destroyed for decades. Yet, despite the enormity of the task, he didn't delay. He took immediate action.

In **Nehemiah 2:17**, Nehemiah says to the people of Jerusalem, **"You see the trouble we are in, how Jerusalem lies in ruins, with its gates burned. Come, let us build the wall of Jerusalem**, that we may no longer suffer derision." Here, he didn't offer excuses; he simply acknowledged the problem and called the people to action. This is often the first step in our own journey of restoration: moving past procrastination and into action.

Procrastination is a major barrier that prevents many from taking the first step toward restoration. The fear of failure, feelings of inadequacy, and the uncertainty of how the process will unfold all contribute to putting off important decisions.

However, the truth is that the longer we delay, the further we distance ourselves from the healing and restoration we need.

To overcome procrastination, it's essential to:

- **Set Small, Achievable Goals**
  In Nehemiah's case, he didn't expect the people to rebuild the entire wall at once. Instead, they worked in sections. Similarly, in your own restoration journey, break your goals down into manageable chunks.
  Example: If you're looking to rebuild your health, start by committing to exercise for 15 minutes each day before increasing the duration.

- **Focus on the 'Why'**
  Nehemiah's vision was clear: to restore the identity and dignity of the people. When you have a compelling 'why,' it becomes easier to overcome the inertia of procrastination.
  Example: Remembering why you want to restore a broken relationship or rebuild your financial security can fuel your determination.

- **Take Action, Even If It's Small**
  Sometimes, the hardest part is starting. Taking even one small step can build momentum and break the cycle of inaction.
  Example: If you're struggling with spiritual renewal, start by setting aside five minutes of quiet time each day for prayer or reflection.

By taking action, you make a statement that you are serious about your restoration.

Nehemiah knew that if the people could see that the work was happening, they would be more likely to get involved themselves.

b. The Power of Community

Building Together

One of the most striking features of Nehemiah's rebuilding project is that it wasn't a solitary effort. In **Nehemiah 3**, we see a long list of people, from priests to perfumers to merchants, working together, each contributing to the restoration of the wall. Every person had a role to play, and each contribution was essential. This chapter underscores the importance of **community** in the process of rebuilding.

The wall was not rebuilt by Nehemiah alone—it took a collective effort. The people who participated in rebuilding the wall each worked on the section closest to them, forming a chain of labor that ultimately resulted in the completion of the entire wall.

This principle applies to our personal restoration as well. Whether it's restoring relationships, healing from a difficult season, or rebuilding our personal goals, we don't have to do it alone. Surrounding ourselves with supportive, like-minded individuals can make all the difference.

Consider the following points for building a supportive community in your restoration journey:

- **Seek Accountability**
  Nehemiah's workers were all accountable to one another as they rebuilt the wall. Similarly, accountability partners, mentors, or small groups can help keep you on track.
  Example: If you're trying to rebuild your finances, consider finding an accountability partner to check in with regularly about your progress.

- **Share the Burden**
  In **Galatians 6:2**, we are called to "bear one another's burdens, and so fulfill the law of Christ." This is exactly what Nehemiah did — he organized people to work together and encouraged them when they were discouraged.
  Example: If you're struggling in a relationship, find a counselor, pastor, or friend who can walk with you through the healing process.

- **Celebrate Small Wins**
  Every time a section of the wall was completed, the people celebrated. As you work toward your restoration, take time to acknowledge and celebrate the progress you make, no matter how small.
  Example: Celebrate the achievement of a new healthy habit or the progress made in rebuilding trust with someone.

c. Overcoming Opposition

Working Through Challenges

No great rebuilding project is without opposition, and Nehemiah faced his fair share of enemies. In **Nehemiah 4**, we see how his enemies—Sanballat, Tobiah, and others—mocked, ridiculed, and even threatened the workers. However, Nehemiah didn't let this deter him.

He responded with courage, wisdom, and strategic planning. He stationed guards to protect the workers and encouraged the people to keep going despite the threats.

When we embark on a journey of restoration, we should expect challenges. Whether these challenges come in the form of **external opposition** (like discouragement from others) or **internal opposition** (like self-doubt or fear), they can often feel overwhelming. However, just as Nehemiah did, we must learn to respond to opposition with courage and resolve.

Here's how we can overcome opposition during our restoration journey:

- **Keep Your Focus on the Goal**
  Nehemiah's focus was unwavering: rebuild the wall to restore the dignity and safety of the people. When we are clear about our ultimate goal, external distractions and discouragement become less significant.
  Example: If someone discourages your attempt to

rebuild a broken relationship, remind yourself of the deeper purpose: healing and reconciliation.

- **Defend Your Progress**
  In **Nehemiah 4:16-18**, Nehemiah placed guards to protect the workers and encouraged them to defend their work. As you rebuild, protect the progress you make by guarding your time, energy, and focus.
  Example: If you're working on rebuilding your spiritual life, defend it by prioritizing time with God and avoiding distractions that draw you away.

- **Trust God's Provision**
  In **Nehemiah 4:20**, Nehemiah says, "Our God will fight for us." In the face of opposition, we can find strength in knowing that God is with us. He will fight on our behalf and provide the resources we need to continue the work.
  Example: When you're tempted to give up, remind yourself that God is with you in the process and that His strength is made perfect in your weakness (2 Corinthians 12:9).

d. Seeing the Project Through

Persevering with Patience

Restoration is often a long, arduous journey. Nehemiah's team worked tirelessly, often under threat, but they didn't give up. In **Nehemiah 6:15**, after facing intense opposition and threats, the wall was finally completed. The perseverance of the workers, fueled by their faith in God and their commitment to the cause, brought about the desired outcome.

Patience is key to completing the work of restoration. The journey may be longer than anticipated, but the perseverance we build along the way deepens our character and strengthens our resolve.

- **Be Patient with Yourself**
  Restoration doesn't happen overnight. Give yourself grace as you work toward rebuilding and don't be discouraged by setbacks.
  Example: If you experience a relapse in your healing or a delay in achieving your goal, remember that growth takes time.

- **Celebrate Progress, Not Perfection**
  Focus on progress rather than perfection. Every step you take toward rebuilding is a victory, even if the goal is not yet fully realized.
  Example: Celebrate each small victory in your restoration process, whether it's a new habit, a healed relationship, or personal growth.

Nehemiah's journey shows us that restoration requires purposeful, faith-driven action. The rebuilding of Jerusalem's walls was a monumental task, but Nehemiah and the people succeeded by acting with perseverance and faith. They didn't allow the enormity of the work to overwhelm them; instead, they took intentional steps forward, inspiring one another to stay committed. Their success is a testament to the power of aligning our actions with God's will and trusting in His guidance. In your own restoration journey, start with small, deliberate steps, and surround yourself with a supportive community.

Like Nehemiah, enlist others who can walk alongside you, offering wisdom and encouragement. Stand firm in the face of opposition, knowing that challenges are part of the process. Rely on God's strength to overcome fear, doubt, and criticism. Trust in His timing, celebrate small victories, and remain consistent, knowing that what you are building is meaningful and lasting.

When you take that first step, you are partnering with God in His great work of restoration. This is not a journey you take alone; God walks with you, providing strength and guidance at every stage. Trust in His promises, persevere in faith, and know that the work you are doing is creating a legacy of hope and purpose.

Chapter IV

Watch Out For Enemies

Identifying and Overcoming Opposition.

One of the undeniable truths of any significant rebuilding process is that there will always be opposition. Whether you're working to restore your spiritual life, relationships, finances, or health, you will face challenges—some external and others internal—that will try to derail your efforts. Nehemiah's journey is a powerful reminder of how we must be vigilant and prepared to face both external and internal enemies that will attempt to stop the work of restoration.

In **Nehemiah 4**, we see that the rebuilding efforts of Nehemiah and his people were met with mockery, ridicule, and outright threats from external enemies like Sanballat and Tobiah. They didn't simply criticize the work; they sought to instill fear, confusion, and discouragement in the people. Similarly, as we strive to rebuild and restore various areas of our lives, we will face challenges that attempt to weaken our resolve. These "enemies" may manifest in many forms, such as people who criticize our progress, internal self-doubt, or even spiritual warfare.

"When Sanballat heard that we were rebuilding the wall, he became angry and was greatly incensed.

He ridiculed the Jews, and in the presence of his associates and the army of Samaria, he said, 'What are those feeble Jews doing? Will they restore their wall? Will they offer sacrifices? Will they finish in a day? Can they bring the stones back to life from those heaps of rubble—burned as they are?'" (Nehemiah 4:1-2, NIV)

Sanballat's ridicule was meant to undermine the people's confidence and distract them from their task. Nehemiah's response, however, is a model of how to deal with opposition and stay focused on the goal.

In this chapter, we will explore the types of enemies you might face in your own journey of restoration—both external and internal—and how you can overcome them by staying focused on your goal, trusting in God's protection, and using wisdom to navigate challenges.

a. External Enemies

Overcoming Ridicule and Opposition

In **Nehemiah 4:1-3**, Sanballat and Tobiah mocked the people's efforts, questioning their ability to rebuild the walls. These external enemies sought to weaken the morale of the workers by ridiculing their plans and belittling their capabilities.

Ridicule and mockery are common weapons that the enemy uses to discourage people, whether it comes from naysayers or even from people who claim to be well-meaning but do not understand your vision or the work you are doing.

Dealing with External Enemies:

- **Recognize that Opposition is Part of the Process**
  In Nehemiah's case, the opposition did not come as a surprise. He had prepared himself spiritually and emotionally to face the difficulties ahead. When you encounter criticism or mockery, understand that it is part of the journey. **John 15:20** tells us that, "If they persecuted me, they will persecute you." Just as Jesus faced opposition, we, too, will face challenges when we step out in faith to restore what's been broken in our lives.

Example: If you're rebuilding your finances and others mock your effort to budget or pay down debt, remember that their criticism is often based on their own limitations, not on your ability to succeed.

- **Refuse to Be Distracted by Ridicule**
  Nehemiah did not allow the mockery of his enemies to derail him. In fact, when they ridiculed the Jews, he responded with prayer and a renewed commitment to the task at hand. In **Nehemiah 4:4-5**, he immediately brought the matter before God:
  "Hear us, our God, for we are despised. Turn their insults back on their own heads. Give them over as plunder in a land of captivity." Instead of engaging with the critics, Nehemiah took the matter to God.

How to Deal with Ridicule:

  o Stay focused on your purpose and goals.

- Don't get distracted by negative comments; instead, take your concerns to God in prayer.
- Respond with quiet determination, knowing that your work has eternal value.

- **Ignore the Fear of "What ifs"**
In verse 2, Sanballat says, "Will they restore their wall? Will they offer sacrifices? Will they finish in a day?" These kinds of questions — "What if it fails?" or "What if I can't finish?" — can paralyze us with fear. Nehemiah did not entertain such questions. Instead of dwelling on the "what-ifs," he kept his eyes on the prize and continued to work.

Example: If you're struggling with a physical health goal and people mock or question whether you can make lasting changes, remember that your health is worth the effort.

Do not let the fear of failure stop you from starting or continuing.

---

b. Internal Enemies

Overcoming Fear, Doubt, and Discouragement

External enemies are not the only threat to our restoration journey. Sometimes, the most formidable adversaries come from within ourselves—fear, doubt, insecurity, and discouragement. In **Nehemiah 4:10**, the workers themselves began to express concerns:

"The strength of the laborers is giving out, and there is so much rubble that we cannot rebuild the wall."

Even though Nehemiah had motivated the people to start the work, they too began to feel the strain of the task. The rubble was overwhelming, and they began to question if the project could ever be completed.

Internal enemies like **fear and self-doubt** often arise when the task seems too big or the obstacles too great. When we are overwhelmed by the enormity of our goals, we may be tempted to give up.

Dealing with Internal Enemies:

- **Refuse to Let Fear Control You**
  Nehemiah acknowledged the workers' fears, but he didn't allow them to dictate the course of the project. Instead, he spoke words of encouragement and reminded the people that God was with them. In **Nehemiah 4:14**, Nehemiah said, "Don't be afraid of them. Remember the Lord, who is great and awesome, and fight for your families, your sons and your daughters, your wives and your homes."

How to Overcome Fear:

- Remind yourself of God's promises. He is with you in the struggle.

- Surround yourself with voices of encouragement—friends, family, and fellow believers.

- Break the task down into manageable steps to reduce overwhelm.

- **Focus on the Bigger Picture**
When the workers were discouraged, Nehemiah reminded them of the purpose behind the project. Restoration was not just about rebuilding walls; it was about protecting the lives of their families and restoring the glory of God. In moments of discouragement, it is essential to refocus on the bigger picture of why we are rebuilding. For me, this has often meant looking beyond the immediate challenge and reminding myself of the long-term rewards and purpose behind the restoration.

Example: If you're rebuilding a relationship, focus on the healing and restoration it will bring to both you and the other person. Rebuilding your health may not be easy, but remember the goal of feeling strong and vibrant again.

- **Persevere with Patience and Faith**
Even when the task seems too big or when the

progress is slow, patience and perseverance will see us through. Nehemiah encouraged the people to keep working, even when they didn't feel like they could continue. In **Nehemiah 4:21**, the workers "continued the work with half the men holding spears, from the first light of dawn till the stars came out." They didn't give up; they persevered with faith.

How to Persevere:

- Set daily or weekly goals to break down the work into smaller, achievable tasks.
- Celebrate small victories to maintain motivation.
- Trust that God is working in you and through you, even when progress feels slow.

Protection and Guarding the Work

As Nehemiah continued the rebuilding project, he also took practical steps to guard the work from external and internal threats. He stationed armed guards at the most vulnerable points in the wall, and the workers alternated between building and standing guard. **Nehemiah 4:16-18** illustrates this perfectly:

"From that day on, half of my men did the work, while the other half were equipped with spears, shields, bows and armor."

The principle here is clear: while we are engaged in the work of restoration, we must also protect it. Protect your efforts by guarding your time, energy, and focus. **Nehemiah 4:9** tells us, "But we prayed to our God and posted a guard day and night to meet this threat." Prayer and practical protection go hand-in-hand when overcoming opposition.

The road to restoration is rarely smooth. You will face opposition, both from external enemies who seek to discourage and distract you, and from internal enemies like fear, doubt, and discouragement. Nehemiah's story is a powerful reminder that we can overcome these challenges by staying focused on our purpose, praying for God's protection, and continuing to work diligently. Through perseverance, faith, and a willingness to protect our progress, we can overcome any opposition that comes our way.

c. Kick out your Jonah

In the journey of restoration, one of the most challenging aspects is identifying and addressing the "Jonah" in our lives. This is because the Jonah types of enemies can be either external or internal—those destructive habits, attitudes, toxic people, environments, connections.... or decisions that create chaos and prevent progress.

Jonah's story, as told in the book of Jonah, provides a powerful metaphor for how carrying unnecessary burdens or avoiding accountability can sink our efforts at rebuilding and restoration.

THE STORY OF JONAH:
A Lesson in Accountability

Jonah was a prophet who chose to run away from God's instructions.

Instead of going to Nineveh, where God had sent him, Jonah boarded a ship heading in the opposite direction. As they sailed, a powerful storm arose, threatening to destroy the ship. The terrified crew threw their cargo overboard to lighten the load, but the storm raged on. Eventually, Jonah confessed that he was the cause of their troubles:

"Pick me up and throw me into the sea," he replied, "and it will become calm. I know that it is my fault that this great storm has come upon you." (Jonah 1:12, NIV)

When Jonah was thrown into the sea, the storm ceased, and the waters became calm. This story teaches us a profound truth: the chaos in our lives may sometimes be the result of a "Jonah" we are holding onto—be it a toxic habit, unhealthy relationship, or poor decision. Often, instead of addressing the root cause, we make sacrifices elsewhere, just like the crew who tossed their goods overboard. If they had known Jonah was the source of the problem, they would not have wasted their resources.

IDENTIFYING YOUR JONAH

Sometimes, we carry "Jonahs" in our lives without realizing their impact.

These can take many forms:

Poor Financial Decisions: Are you holding onto the Jonah of hire purchase, accumulating liabilities that drain your resources? It's time to evaluate your spending habits and prioritize financial stability.

Unproductive Habits: Perhaps you've developed a pattern of procrastination or poor time management. These habits may seem small but can have a significant cumulative effect.

Toxic Relationships: Are you maintaining connections that hinder your growth or restoration? Sometimes, letting go is necessary for progress.

Avoiding Responsibility: Blaming others—your partner, circumstances, or even trivial excuses like "my dog ate my homework"—is a way of avoiding personal accountability. Recognizing your role in your challenges is essential for true restoration.

When you carry a Jonah, you'll find yourself repeating the same struggles year after year. As the saying goes, "A tree produces fruit after its own kind." If you plant seeds of poor decisions and avoid accountability, you cannot expect a harvest of success and peace.

TAKING ACTION:
Throwing Jonah Overboard

This year, make the decision to confront your Jonah and remove it from your life. Consider these steps:

- 1. **Self-Reflection:** Take a moment to evaluate your life. Ask yourself:

  ✓ Where am I standing today?
  ✓ What are my accomplishments and achievements?
  ✓ What habits, attitudes, or relationships are holding me back?

- 2. **Take Responsibility:** Stop looking for scapegoats. Admit your faults and commit to change. Blaming external factors will only prolong your struggles. Jonah wasn't the merchandise that was thrown overboard—he was the real problem.

Do not be like a horse or a mule, which have no understanding but must be controlled by bit and bridle." (Psalm 32:9, NIV)

- **3. Make Wise Decisions:** Wisdom doesn't require genius—only intentionality.

This year, focus on making thoughtful, deliberate choices. Avoid amassing liabilities or engaging in actions that don't align with your goals.

- **4. Change Your Mentality:** Real, lasting change comes from within. Attend deliverance services, seek mentorship, or pray for guidance, but remember that without a genuine change in mindset, the effort will be in vain.

- **5. Embrace Courage:** Letting go of your Jonah requires courage. It might mean parting with something or someone you've held onto for years, but it's a necessary step toward restoration.

The Consequences of Holding Onto Jonah

When you refuse to address the Jonah in your life, you risk allowing your struggles to follow you into the future. The failures of 2024—or any past year or season—don't have to define your present or your future. Holding onto destructive habits or mindsets will only drag you down further, like a sinking ship filling with water.

No matter how many prayers or deliverance services you attend, if you don't take responsibility and kick Jonah out, your boat will continue to fill with the bitter waters of despair. This is the year to reclaim control of your life. Don't let this year look like the last, filled with the same mistakes, struggles, or regrets. Instead, make a conscious decision to:

The passengers on Jonah's boat found peace and safety only after they threw him into the sea. In the same way, you'll find calm and restoration when you confront and remove the things that are causing chaos in your life.

Therefore, if anyone is in Christ, the new creation has come: The old has gone, the new is here!" (2 Corinthians 5:17, NIV)

Let this year or period be the beginning of a new chapter—a year of restoration, peace, and success. Don't let fear or complacency keep you tied to your Jonah. Take the bold step to throw it overboard, and watch as calm returns to your life.

Kick your Jonah out! It's time to rise up and build a life that reflects God's purpose and plans for you. As you face your own challenges, remember that the work of restoration is worth it. Guard your heart, stay committed, and trust that God is with you every step of the way.

Chapter V

Building Momentum

Strengthening Your Foundations.

Rise up and Build

In Nehemiah's story, the rebuilding of the walls of Jerusalem was not just about erecting physical barriers; it was also about strengthening the foundation of a community. Once the physical work had begun, Nehemiah and the people needed to build momentum to keep the project moving forward.

Momentum is key in any restoration process — whether you are rebuilding your spiritual life, health, relationships, or finances. It is the energy and drive that keeps you going even when the going gets tough. In **Nehemiah 6:15**, after facing intense opposition and adversity, the wall of Jerusalem was finally completed: **"So the wall was completed on the twenty-fifth of Elul, in fifty-two days." (Nehemiah 6:15, NIV)**

In just 52 days, a seemingly impossible task had been completed. The people's ability to build momentum — despite threats, ridicule, and discouragement — was crucial to the success of the rebuilding effort. The same can be said for any restoration journey. Momentum not only ensures that we continue our work, but it also strengthens the foundation of what we are building.

This chapter will explore how to build and maintain momentum in the restoration process and how to strengthen the foundation of your efforts.

a. Strong Foundation

The Importance of a Strong Foundation

Before any significant building project can take place, the foundation must be laid.

In Nehemiah's case, the initial step of rebuilding the walls began with gathering the resources, assigning work, and organizing the labor force. But before any walls could be built, the foundation had to be secure. Without a strong foundation, even the most well-intentioned efforts will fall short.

Jesus also emphasized the importance of building on a solid foundation in **Matthew 7:24-27** when He compared wise builders to those who built their houses on rock instead of sand:

"Everyone who hears these words of mine and does them will be like a wise man who built his house on the rock. And the rain fell, and the floods came, and the winds blew and beat on that house, but it did not fall, because it had been founded on the rock." (Matthew 7:24-25, ESV)

Building momentum in restoration requires us to first ensure that we are building on a strong foundation.

This foundation is not only about practical skills, but also about a deep spiritual grounding. Whether you are working to rebuild a relationship, financial stability, or your health, it is crucial to establish a solid base upon which to build. That foundation should be centered on:

- **Faith in God's Promise of Restoration**
  In **Joel 2:25**, God promises to restore the years that have been lost:

"I will restore to you the years that the swarming locust has eaten."

Understanding that God is the ultimate source of your restoration will help you build your efforts on the unshakable foundation of His faithfulness.

- **Clear Goals and Intentions**
  Nehemiah's initial step was to identify the goal: rebuilding the walls of Jerusalem for the protection and restoration of the people. Your foundation should include clear, well-defined goals for what you are seeking to restore. Whether it's physical health, emotional healing, or financial stability, knowing exactly what you want to accomplish helps you stay grounded and focused.

- **Support Systems**
  Nehemiah built a team to support him in the restoration process. In your own restoration journey, a strong foundation includes having a community of people who will help hold you accountable, encourage you when you grow weary, and offer wisdom and perspective. As Ecclesiastes 4:9-10 says,

"Two are better than one, because they have a good reward for their toil. For if they fall, one will lift up his fellow."

Once your foundation is set, you can begin to build momentum.

b. Taking Consistent Action

Building Momentum

Once the foundation is in place, the work of restoration begins in earnest. Building momentum is like gathering speed on a journey—it requires consistent action and effort, even when progress seems slow. **Nehemiah 3** provides a model of how consistent, coordinated action can lead to remarkable results.

In this chapter, Nehemiah organizes the people, assigns each group of workers a specific section of the wall to rebuild, and they begin working in earnest. The momentum was built by each person doing their part, day after day. As a result, the work that might have seemed impossible was accomplished in just 52 days.

The key to building momentum in your own restoration efforts is:

- **Consistency Over Intensity**
Nehemiah didn't expect the workers to rebuild the

entire wall in one day. Instead, the project was divided into manageable sections, and the workers were encouraged to complete their portions one step at a time. The restoration process is about the steady accumulation of small, consistent actions that build upon each other.
Example: If you're rebuilding your health, start by committing to small, consistent habits, like walking 15 minutes a day or cutting back on sugar. Gradually, these small habits will compound into lasting results.

- **Celebrate Small Wins**
  As each section of the wall was completed, Nehemiah and the people celebrated their progress. In the restoration process, it is easy to become discouraged if we only focus on the end goal. Celebrating small wins along the way will keep you motivated and energized.
  Example: If you're restoring a relationship, celebrate every step forward — whether it's a meaningful conversation, an act of kindness, or a commitment to communication.

- **Remain Flexible**
  Even when building momentum, unexpected challenges can arise. In **Nehemiah 4:7-9**, when opposition came against the people, Nehemiah adapted by posting guards to protect the workers. In your journey of restoration, obstacles will arise, and you may need to adjust your plans to

accommodate new circumstances.

Example: If your health journey is interrupted by a setback, such as an illness, don't give up. Adjust your routine to accommodate your body's needs and get back on track as soon as possible.

"And I am sure of this, that he who began a good work in you will bring it to completion at the day of Jesus Christ." Trust that God is faithful to bring the work of restoration to completion in your life.

c. Overcoming Setbacks

Maintaining Momentum in the Face of Opposition

Even when momentum is building, opposition can slow or derail progress.

In **Nehemiah 4**, when Sanballat and Tobiah sought to discourage the workers, the people grew weary. The task seemed overwhelming, and there was talk of giving up. But Nehemiah refused to let the opposition prevent progress. Instead, he prayed, encouraged the people, and implemented practical solutions to protect the workers (Nehemiah 4:13-18).

Overcoming setbacks and maintaining momentum requires resilience. It means not letting challenges — whether internal or external — stop you from moving forward.

Here's how to keep building momentum when setbacks arise:

- **Shift Your Perspective**
  In times of discouragement, Nehemiah reminded the workers of the bigger picture. The work they were doing was not just about rebuilding walls — it was about restoring the dignity and safety of their community. When you face setbacks, focus on your ultimate purpose and the reason behind your restoration.
  Example: If you're rebuilding your finances, focus on the end goal: financial freedom and the ability to live without debt. This will keep you motivated when the process feels slow.

Building Lasting Momentum

Momentum is the driving force that propels us forward in any restoration journey. Nehemiah's story shows us that when we build on a strong foundation, take consistent action, celebrate small wins, and overcome setbacks, we can achieve remarkable progress — even in the face of challenges.

In your own life, as you seek to restore what's been broken or lost, remember that momentum is not just about speed — it's about persistence and consistency.

Chapter VI

The Final Touches

Refining and Perfecting.

After Nehemiah and the people of Jerusalem completed the wall in just 52 days, the project wasn't over. They had done the heavy lifting, but the task of refining, perfecting, and preparing for the future remained. This final stage of the restoration process, much like the final touches on a home or a work of art, is about attention to detail, finishing strong, and ensuring that the work done has lasting impact.

Just as Nehemiah took steps to finalize the rebuilding of the wall, so too must we focus on refining and perfecting the work God has called us to do in our lives.

In **Nehemiah 7:1,** Nehemiah says, **"After the wall had been rebuilt and I had set the doors in place, the gatekeepers, the musicians, and the Levites were appointed."** Nehemiah didn't simply declare the work complete after the physical walls were restored. He knew that the completion of the walls wasn't the end of the process—it was just the beginning of a new era of protection, prosperity, and spiritual renewal for the people of Jerusalem.

To ensure that the city would thrive, Nehemiah focused on securing its internal operations, establishing leadership, and creating systems to maintain and care for the restored city.

The same is true in our own restoration journeys. After the heavy lifting is done—whether it's the restoration of relationships, health, finances, or personal growth—we must focus on the **final touches** to ensure sustainability. This chapter will explore the importance of refinement in the restoration process and how to apply final touches to secure long-lasting transformation.

a. Attention to Detail

Refining the Work – Attention to Detail

When Nehemiah completed the physical rebuilding of the wall, he didn't immediately move on to the next project. He took the time to ensure that all aspects of the work were aligned with the vision God had given him. Similarly, after embarking on a journey of restoration, it's essential to pay attention to the smaller, often overlooked details.

Refinement is the process of improving and perfecting something that has already been created. It's about making small, thoughtful adjustments that contribute to the overall quality of the work.

The Bible speaks to this refining process in **Proverbs 4:23**, where it says, **"Above all else, guard your heart, for everything you do flows from it."**

Just as Nehemiah ensured that the wall's final gates were securely in place, we need to ensure that our own hearts are protected and aligned with God's will. If our hearts aren't protected, our work—whether in relationships, finances, or other areas—will be compromised.

How to Refine and Perfect Your Restoration Efforts:

- **Identify Areas of Weakness**
  Just as Nehemiah appointed gatekeepers and Levites to safeguard the city (Nehemiah 7:1), we must identify any areas of weakness in our own restoration efforts. Are there areas where you've been neglecting your growth or allowing negative influences to enter?
  Example: If you've been restoring a relationship but notice patterns of poor communication resurfacing, refining the work may mean learning better communication strategies or addressing unresolved issues.

- **Implement Protective Measures**
  Nehemiah made sure that the city's gatekeepers were assigned to prevent unwanted interruptions (Nehemiah 7:1). Similarly, after working hard to restore an area of your life, you need to establish boundaries that protect your progress.
  Example: If you've restored your health after a period of unhealthy living, continue protecting your well-being by setting boundaries around food choices, exercise, and stress management.

- **Celebrate Completion, But Focus on Sustainability**
  The act of completing a goal is important, but true

success comes when we build sustainable practices to maintain that goal. Refining the work means evaluating how to keep the momentum going long-term.

Example: After restoring your finances, don't simply return to old spending habits. Commit to a sustainable budgeting plan to ensure long-term financial health.

b. Adding the Finishing Touches

Perfecting the Work – Adding the Finishing Touches

Once the major work of restoration has been done, the next step is perfecting the details. In Nehemiah's case, he didn't just build the walls and walk away. He ensured the gates were functional, and he appointed trustworthy leaders to take care of the city (Nehemiah 7:1). Similarly, we must perfect the work by adding small details that reflect the value of what has been restored.

In **Colossians 3:23**, Paul encourages us to approach our work with excellence:

"Whatever you do, work heartily, as for the Lord and not for men."

The work we do—whether it's in our relationships, health, finances, or personal development—deserves to be approached with the same care and attention to detail that

Nehemiah gave the restoration of Jerusalem's walls. **Perfection** doesn't mean flawless execution, but it does mean giving our best effort and honoring God in the process.

How to Add the Finishing Touches in Your Restoration:

- **Establish Systems of Accountability**
  In Nehemiah's time, he appointed gatekeepers and officers to ensure the walls and the city functioned smoothly (Nehemiah 7:1-2). For us, creating systems of accountability helps keep the restoration process in check.
  Example: If you've restored your health, establish a system of accountability, whether it's with a friend or a personal health coach, to keep you on track.

- **Create Routines for Maintenance**
  Nehemiah didn't simply restore the walls and leave them unattended; he created a plan to ensure the ongoing safety and vitality of the city. Similarly, in our restoration journeys, we need to establish routines that allow us to continue thriving.
  Example: After restoring your finances, establish a monthly routine of reviewing your budget and making adjustments as needed.

c. Spiritual Refinement

Strengthening Your Relationship with God

One of the most important aspects of refinement and perfection is the spiritual element. Restoration is not just about improving external circumstances, but also about deepening our relationship with God. Nehemiah's leadership was deeply rooted in his faith, and his actions were guided by prayer and reliance on God's provision.

As we seek to refine and perfect the work of restoration, we must also focus on strengthening our relationship with God. In **Psalm 51:10**, David prays, **"Create in me a clean heart, O God, and renew a right spirit within me."**

Spiritual refinement involves continually seeking God's guidance, keeping our hearts aligned with His will, and allowing Him to cleanse and renew us. As you focus on refining the restoration efforts in your life, remember that the most important work is the work that God does within you.

How to Refine Your Spiritual Life:

- **Prioritize Time with God**
  The more time we spend with God, the more refined and aligned we become with His will. Spend time in prayer, worship, and studying His Word.
  Example: If you've restored your emotional health, don't neglect your spiritual health. Set aside time each day for prayer and reflection to stay grounded.

- **Seek God's Guidance for Next Steps**
  Just as Nehemiah sought God's direction at every

critical juncture in his journey, we too must seek God's guidance when moving forward in our restoration.
Example: Before making a major decision in your life—whether it's about your career, relationships, or health—take time to pray and ask God for wisdom.

- **Allow God to Perfect You**
  Restoration doesn't stop with us—it's also about allowing God to continue His work in our lives. Just as Nehemiah was committed to restoring the physical walls of Jerusalem, God is committed to perfecting the spiritual walls of our hearts in the name of Jesus.
  Example: Even if you've made progress in an area of your life, don't become complacent. Ask God to continue refining and perfecting you.

The Celebration of Completion

Once the final touches have been applied, it's important to celebrate the progress and the work that's been done. Nehemiah didn't just finish the restoration and walk away. In **Nehemiah 12:27-43**, he led the people in a great celebration of the completed work. They rejoiced, sang songs of praise, and gave thanks to God for His faithfulness. Likewise, we must take time to celebrate the restoration in our lives.

The illustration symbolizes the triumphant completion of a restoration journey, capturing the essence of faith, perseverance, and divine guidance. The ancient wall, once in ruins, now stands tall as scaffolding is removed, signifying the final stages of hard-earned success. Workers rejoice, representing the collective effort and unity required to achieve meaningful progress. In the foreground, a figure in traditional robes kneels in gratitude, offering prayers of thanksgiving to God for His faithfulness throughout the journey. The glowing sunrise in the background embodies new beginnings, hope, and the promise of future blessings as the restoration marks not just an end, but a new chapter.

Celebrate the hard work, the perseverance, and the victories—no matter how big or small. This celebration acknowledges that we have walked through the process with God's help and that He has been faithful to complete the work.

How to Celebrate Your Restoration:

- **Give Thanks**
  Like Nehemiah and the people of Jerusalem, express your gratitude to God for His help and faithfulness throughout the restoration process.

- **Share Your Story**
  Celebrating also involves sharing your testimony with others. Share how God has restored and

renewed you to encourage others in their own journeys.

The final touches on any restoration process are not just about finishing the work — they are about making sure the work lasts.

The enemy is not attacking you because you are weak; he is attacking because you are a threat. There is something powerful inside you, and he knows it. Thieves don't break into empty houses. The enemy couldn't defeat you, so now he's trying to wear you down. But don't give in. The tide is about to turn in your favor. God sees your struggles. He knows your heart. He sees how tired you are, but He is not finished with you yet. Keep Him first. Trust Him, even when the way forward seems unclear — He is already making a way for you. He is with you, He is for you, and He is working everything for your good. Keep moving forward, because your breakthrough is closer than you think.

Chapter VII

Faithful Finishing

Completing What You Started.

Restoration doesn't end when the walls are partially built or when we feel like we've regained "enough" stability. True restoration is complete when the vision is fully realized. Nehemiah didn't stop when the walls were halfway constructed, nor did he allow distractions to delay the project. He understood that starting was important, but finishing strong was critical.

"I have fought the good fight, I have finished the race, I have kept the faith." (2 Timothy 4:7, NIV)

In this final chapter, we will explore the discipline of finishing what you started and the spiritual significance of seeing things through. The completion of the walls of Jerusalem wasn't just a victory for Nehemiah and the people — it was a testament to their perseverance and their partnership with God. It symbolized divine restoration and a new season of security and hope.

1. Stay Focused Until the End

Nehemiah's enemies didn't stop their attacks simply because the walls were close to completion. Instead, their opposition intensified as the work neared the finish line. They tried to distract Nehemiah with meetings and false accusations, but he remained steadfast. He famously responded:

"I am doing a great work and I cannot come down." (Nehemiah 6:3, ESV)

In your restoration journey, distractions and obstacles may increase as you approach your goal. Old habits, doubts, and external challenges may try to derail you. But like Nehemiah, you must recognize the importance of your work and stay committed to finishing it. Don't come down from the wall. Stay focused.

Practical Steps to Maintain Focus:
- Set clear milestones and celebrate small victories along the way.
- Keep a daily or weekly journal to track your progress and reflect on God's faithfulness.
- Eliminate unnecessary distractions and prioritize tasks that move you closer to completion.

---

2. Overcome the Fear of Completion

Sometimes, fear of the unknown can prevent us from finishing what we've started. What happens after the restoration is complete? What if things fall apart again? These questions can create hesitation and self-doubt, but it's important to remember that God's provision doesn't end when the work is done. In fact, it's just the beginning of new blessings and responsibilities.

God didn't leave Nehemiah once the walls were rebuilt. Instead, He continued to provide guidance as Nehemiah established reforms and strengthened the community. In the same way, God will continue to walk with you beyond your season of rebuilding.

> "Being confident of this, that he who began a good work in you will carry it on to completion until the day of Christ Jesus." (Philippians 1:6, NIV)

Finishing isn't a sign that the journey is over—it's an indication that you're stepping into a new chapter. Trust that God has already prepared the next steps for you.

---

3. Finish with Integrity

When you reach the final stages of restoration, it's tempting to cut corners or rush the process just to be "done." But true restoration requires integrity. Nehemiah didn't compromise on the quality of the work, and neither should you. He ensured that the gates were securely in place and that the people were ready to defend what they had built.

Integrity means finishing well, even if it takes longer than expected. It means honoring the process, trusting God's timing, and ensuring that what you build will stand the test of time.

> **"Unless the Lord builds the house, the builders labor in vain." (Psalm 127:1, NIV)**

Be faithful in the details. The foundation you lay now will determine the strength of what you've built. Whether you're rebuilding your faith, relationships, or dreams, finish with excellence and dedication.

4. Dedicate Your Restoration to God

Once the walls of Jerusalem were completed, Nehemiah and the people celebrated with joy and dedicated their work to God through praise, worship, and thanksgiving. They recognized that their success was not solely due to their efforts but was made possible by God's grace and intervention.

In your own journey, take time to give thanks and dedicate the completion of your restoration to God. This can be through prayer, worship, or even sharing your testimony with others. Acknowledge that He has been with you every step of the way, providing strength when you felt weak and wisdom when you felt lost.

"Give thanks to the Lord, for he is good; his love endures forever." (Psalm 107:1, NIV)

---

5. Prepare for the Next Chapter

Finishing one season of restoration often marks the beginning of a new chapter. Just as Nehemiah continued to lead and reform the people after the walls were rebuilt, you, too, are stepping into a season of new opportunities and responsibilities. Be ready to build upon what you have restored.

Questions to Consider as You Move Forward:

- What new habits or practices do you need to maintain what you've built?
- How can you protect your progress from future setbacks?
- Who can you mentor or help using the lessons you've learned during your restoration journey?

Remember, your journey doesn't end with the completion of the walls. Restoration is an ongoing process, and God will continue to work through you to bring about His purposes.

You have come so far, and you have done the work. What you have built is meaningful, and it will last. As you stand at the threshold of completion, know that God is pleased with your faithfulness and perseverance. You've trusted Him, worked diligently, and stayed the course.

Celebrate this victory, knowing that it is not just the end of a chapter but the beginning of something greater. Just as Nehemiah and the people rejoiced when the walls were complete, take a moment to rejoice in what you've accomplished. The God who helped you rebuild will be the same God who sustains you as you move forward.

Chapter VIII

Celebration

Acknowledging the Completion.

The work of restoration is not complete until it is celebrated and dedicated to a higher purpose. In Nehemiah's story, after completing the wall, he did not simply declare victory and walk away.

Instead, he led the people in a **celebration** and **dedication** of the completed work.

In **Nehemiah 12:27-43**, we see the people of Jerusalem gathering to celebrate the restoration of the city walls with songs, music, and worship. This celebration was not just a party — it was a way to honor God for His faithfulness in completing the work and to rededicate the city and its people to God's service.

In our own lives, when we experience restoration — whether it's in our health, relationships, finances, or spiritual life — it's important to take time to **acknowledge the completion** of the work and give thanks. Celebrating and dedicating the restored parts of our lives is not just an act of gratitude, but also a way to **mark the transition** to a new season. In this chapter, we will explore the significance of **dedicating** and **celebrating** the work of restoration, acknowledging God's role, and looking ahead to the future with renewed purpose.

The Importance of Celebration

Celebration is a biblical principle that reflects both gratitude and joy. The act of celebrating the completion of a project, especially one as significant as restoration, is an expression of faith. In **Psalm 126:3**, the psalmist declares,

"The Lord has done great things for us, and we are filled with joy."

When God brings restoration into our lives, it is indeed a great thing. The act of celebrating is not only a way to acknowledge the magnitude of what has been done, but it is also a way of publicly declaring that God has been faithful and has brought us through a difficult season. As we celebrate, we remind ourselves of the journey and the lessons we have learned, while also thanking God for His intervention and provision.

Why Celebrating is Important:

- **It Marks a Milestone**
  Celebrating the completion of restoration allows us to mark the milestone in our journey. It's an acknowledgment that we have come through a season of struggle, and God has brought us to a new place of healing and strength.
  Example: If you have rebuilt your health after a long illness or have overcome a financial challenge, celebrating the victory allows you to recognize the hard work and perseverance that brought you through.

- **It Reinforces Gratitude**
  Gratitude is a key component of spiritual growth. By celebrating, we make sure we don't forget the

source of our restoration—God Himself. We also take time to express our thankfulness, which keeps us humble and aware of His goodness.
Example: After restoring your spiritual walk with God, a celebration might involve worshiping God and sharing your testimony with others to encourage them.

- **It Provides a Platform for Testimony**
  Celebrations give us the opportunity to share our stories with others, encouraging them in their own restoration journeys. **Psalm 107:2** says,

"Let the redeemed of the Lord tell their story—those he redeemed from the hand of the foe."

Your restoration journey can inspire others to believe in God's power to heal, restore, and redeem.

Practical Ways to Celebrate Your Restoration:

- **Worship and Praise**
  Just as Nehemiah led the people of Jerusalem in a time of worship and praise after the wall was completed, we can celebrate our restoration by offering worship to God.
  Example: You could spend time in personal worship, or gather with others in your community to thank God for His work in your life.

- **Share Your Story**
  Celebrate by sharing your testimony with others. Whether it's through a conversation, a social

media post, or a written letter, telling others about your restoration encourages them and brings glory to God.
Example: If you have healed from a serious illness, consider sharing your journey with others to encourage those who are still struggling.

- **Reflect and Journal**
Take time to reflect on your journey of restoration by journaling or praying. Write down your feelings of gratitude and the ways in which God has worked in your life. This reflection can help solidify the lessons learned and keep you grounded in the process of healing.
Example: If you've worked on rebuilding a broken relationship, take time to reflect on how far you've come, what you've learned, and what you're grateful for.

Dedication: Giving the Restoration Back to God

Celebration is about **acknowledging** the work done, but **dedication** is about surrendering the completed work to God for His purposes.

In **Nehemiah 12:43**, we read that after the people celebrated the completion of the wall, they "offered great sacrifices, rejoicing because God had given them great joy." This dedication was an act of honoring God for His faithfulness and asking for His continued blessing on the work they had done.

Dedication is about recognizing that the restoration isn't just for our benefit—it's for God's glory and the benefit of others. When we dedicate the restored areas of our lives to God, we are saying, "God, this work is not just for me—it is for Your purpose and Your kingdom."

Why Dedication Matters:

- **It Acknowledges God as the Source**
  Dedication is a way of publicly acknowledging that God is the ultimate source of our restoration. When we dedicate our work back to God, we remind ourselves that He is the One who has provided for us, healed us, and brought us through difficult times.
  Example: If you've restored your finances, dedicating that restoration to God may involve pledging to use your financial resources to support others or contribute to His kingdom.

- **It Secures the Future of the Work**
  Just as Nehemiah dedicated the walls of Jerusalem to God, dedicating the work of restoration in your life ensures that it is not just a temporary fix, but something that will continue to bear fruit. It is a way of inviting God to protect and sustain the work He has done.
  Example: If you've rebuilt a broken relationship,

dedicating that relationship to God may involve committing to ongoing communication, patience, and understanding, with God's help.

- **It Aligns Our Work with God's Greater Purpose**
  When we dedicate our restoration efforts to God, we are aligning ourselves with His greater purposes. We are acknowledging that the work done is part of a larger story of redemption that God is writing in the world.
  Example: If you've restored your health, dedicating it to God might involve using your strength to serve others and glorify Him in your daily life.

How to Dedicate the Restoration Work:

- **Pray of Dedication**
  Offer a prayer of dedication, acknowledging God as the source of your restoration and asking for His continued guidance in maintaining and using what has been restored.
  Example: If you've restored your finances, pray and dedicate your resources to God's purposes, asking for wisdom in how to manage and distribute your wealth.

- **Surrender the Restoration to God**
  Dedication is an act of surrender. Just as the Israelites offered sacrifices to God after the walls were completed, we surrender our completed

work by letting go of control and trusting that God will use it for His glory.

- *Example:* If you've restored a relationship, surrender it to God by praying for His continued healing and allowing Him to guide your interactions and future growth.

- **Live with a Renewed Purpose**
  Dedication isn't just a one-time act—it's a lifestyle. After you dedicate the work to God, live with a renewed sense of purpose, understanding that the restoration you've experienced is a tool for greater service to God and others.
  Example: If you've restored your spiritual walk, live with intentionality, seeking to honor God in all areas of your life and sharing your restored faith with others.

Looking Ahead – New Beginnings

Once we celebrate and dedicate the work of restoration, we must look ahead to the new season that is now unfolding. **Nehemiah 12:44-47** tells us that after the wall was completed and dedicated, the people of Jerusalem began to establish the systems and practices that would ensure the prosperity of the city. The restoration of the walls was just the beginning of a new chapter of flourishing and growth for Jerusalem.

Similarly, once restoration occurs in our lives, it opens the door to new possibilities and opportunities. The journey of restoration is never the end — it is the beginning of a new chapter, a new season of growth, purpose, and impact.

Looking Ahead:

- **Embrace the New Season**
  Celebrate not only the completion of the restoration, but also the beginning of what comes next. Restoration opens doors to new opportunities for growth and service.
  Example: If you've restored a career after a setback, use this new beginning to pursue greater professional goals, bringing glory to God in your work.

- **Invest in Long-Term Flourishing**
  Dedication and celebration are not just about looking back — they are about investing in the future. Continue to nurture the restored areas of your life by maintaining habits, setting new goals, and seeking God's guidance in all things.
  Example: If you've restored your health, make long-term investments in your well-being by establishing routines for exercise, rest, and nutrition.

The journey of restoration culminates in celebration and dedication. Celebrating the work done allows us to honor God and acknowledge the progress we've made. Dedicating the work back to God ensures that the restoration is aligned with His purposes and that it will be sustained for the future.

And looking ahead with a renewed sense of purpose helps us embrace the new season of growth and opportunity that follows.

As you finish your restoration journey, take time to celebrate, dedicate, and look forward with anticipation to all that God has in store for the next chapter.

Remember that restoration is not just about fixing what was broken; it's about moving into a new season of flourishing, purpose, and growth.

Now, we've reached the final stages of restoration, it's essential to remember and affirm who we are in Christ. The Scriptures teach that our identity transcends the physical realm — we are spiritual beings created in the image of God. This understanding is vital for dedicating ourselves fully to God and living out our purpose in this new season of restoration.

a. Understanding your True Identity

The Bible declares that **you are a spirit, living in a body, and possessing a soul**. This truth is foundational. God Himself is spirit, and since you are made in His image, you are a spirit too. Your outward appearance, achievements, or the perceptions of others do not define you. Instead, God defines you based on your inner man — your spirit.

"So God created mankind in his own image, in the image of God he created them; male and female he created them." (Genesis 1:27, NIV)

Your spirit, renewed through Christ, is who you truly are. While people may judge you by external factors, God sees and speaks to your inner man, calling you into His divine purpose. As a child of God, your identity is rooted in the truths of Scripture:

- **You are born again** (John 3:3).
- **You are a new creation** (2 Corinthians 5:17).
- **You are the light of the world** (Matthew 5:14).
- **You are a city on a hill** (Matthew 5:14).
- **You are the salt of the earth** (Matthew 5:13).
- **You are the righteousness of God** (2 Cor. 5:21).
- **You are the glory of God** (John 17:22).
- **You are more than a conqueror** (Rom.8:37).
- **You are born of God** (1 John 5:4).
- **You are the first and not the last** (Deut 28:13).
- **You are above and not beneath** (Deut.28:13).
- **You are an overcomer** (Revelation 12:11).
- **You are a winner by default** (Romans 8:31).
- **You are triumphant** (2 Corinthians 2:14).
- **You are the seed of Abraham** (Galatians 3:29).
- **You are a member of the family of God** (Eph. 2:19).

- **You are a priest** (1 Peter 2:9).
- **You are the image of God** (Genesis 1:27).
- **You are a partaker of the divine nature of God** (2 Pe.1:4).
- **You are a king or queen** (Revelation 1:6).
- **You are God's child** (John 1:12).
- **You are Christ's friend** (John 15:15).
- **You are a member of Christ's Body** (1 Cor. 12:27).

b. Living in your Identity

As you dedicate yourself to God and celebrate the restoration He has brought, it's important to live confidently in your identity as a child of God. This means embracing the following truths about your position and purpose:

- **You are a citizen of heaven** (Philippians 3:20).
- **You are hidden with Christ in God** (Col. 3:3).
- **The evil one cannot touch you** (1 John 5:18).
- **You are blessed with every spiritual blessing** (Eph.1:3).
- **You're chosen before the creation of the world** (Eph. 1:4).
- **You are holy and blameless** (Ephesians 1:4).
- **You are forgiven of every sin** (Ephesians 1:7).
- **You are a saint** (Ephesians 1:1).
- **You are God's co-worker** (2 Corinthians 6:1).
- **You are alive with Christ** (Ephesians 2:5).
- **You are raised up with Christ** (Ephesians 2:6).
- **You're seated with Christ in heavenly places** (Eph.2:6).

- **You are God's workmanship** (Eph. 2:10).

Dedicate yourself to living out these truths as you step into your restored identity. Doing so will enable you to walk in victory, knowing that you are secure in God's promises and empowered by His Spirit.

c. Walking in your Victory

Living in the fullness of your identity means rejecting lies and limitations and embracing your calling as a victorious believer. Consider these additional truths:

- **You are a member of God's household** (Ephesians 2:19).
- **You are secure** (Romans 8:38-39).
- **You are a holy temple** (1 Corinthians 3:16).
- **You are dead to sin** (Romans 6:11).
- **You are not alone** (Hebrews 13:5).
- **You are victorious** (1 Corinthians 15:57).
- **You are chosen and dearly loved** (Col.3:12).
- **You are set free** (Galatians 5:1).
- **You are crucified with Christ** (Gal.2:20).
- **You are part of God's kingdom** (Col.1:13).
- **You are healed from sin** (1 Peter 2:24).
- **You are no longer condemned** (Romans 8:1).
- **You are protected** (Psalm 91:14).
- **You are delivered** (Colossians 1:13).
- **You are redeemed from the curse of the Law** (Gal.3:13).
- **You're qualified to share in His inheritance** (Col. 1:12).

Above all, **you are godlike** in nature because you are made in His image and called to reflect His glory in the world. This is not to say you are divine, but that you are empowered by the divine nature of God to live victoriously and purposefully.

"His divine power has given us everything we need for a godly life through our knowledge of him who called us by his own glory and goodness." (2 Peter 1:3, NIV)

d. A New Mindset for Dedication

As you dedicate yourself to God and celebrate the restoration He has brought into your life, it is crucial to adopt a new mindset—one rooted in faith, identity, and purpose. This new way of thinking is not merely about positive thinking or self-affirmation; it is about seeing yourself through the lens of God's Word and embracing who you truly are in Christ. It's about letting go of old identities shaped by past failures, hurts, and limitations, and stepping boldly into the identity God has given you.

Too often, we allow past mistakes, disappointments, or others' opinions to define us. We look in the mirror and see someone limited by circumstance, unworthy of greatness, or marked by past pain. But God sees beyond all of that. He sees you as redeemed, chosen, loved, and equipped for a divine purpose.

"Therefore, if anyone is in Christ, the new creation has come: The old has gone, the new is here!" (2 Corinthians 5:17, NIV)

Renewing Your Mind for Transformation

The key to this transformation lies in renewing your mind. Paul's instruction to the Romans is clear:

"Do not conform to the pattern of this world, but be transformed by the renewing of your mind. Then you will be able to test and approve what God's will is — his good, pleasing and perfect will." (Romans 12:2, NIV)

This renewed mindset involves a conscious effort to replace worldly thinking with Godly wisdom. It means rejecting lies that say you're not good enough, and instead, declaring the truth of God's Word over your life. It means choosing faith over fear, hope over despair, and purpose over passivity.

Practical Steps to Renew Your Mind:

- ✓ Meditate on God's Word Daily
- ✓ Speak Life
- ✓ Guard Your Mind
- ✓ Practice Gratitude
- ✓ Act in Faith

Stepping Boldly into Your Next Chapter

As you celebrate who you are in Christ, dedicate yourself to living out His purpose, and step boldly into the next chapter of your life, remember that you are not doing this alone. God is with you every step of the way, equipping you, guiding you, and cheering you on. He has already gone before you, preparing a path of victory, fulfillment, and purpose.

Declare these truths over your life:

I am chosen, set apart, and dearly loved (Colossians 3:12).

I am the righteousness of God in Christ Jesus (2 Corinthians 5:21).

I am more than a conqueror through Him who loves me (Romans 8:37).

I am God's masterpiece, created to do good works (Ephesians 2:10).

I am a light in the world, shining God's glory wherever I go (Matthew 5:14).

Bibliography

Biblical References:

- The Holy Bible, New International Version (NIV)
- The Holy Bible, King James Version (KJV)

Primary Scripture Sources:

- Nehemiah 1-6
- Joel 2:25
- Philippians 1:6
- 2 Corinthians 5:17
- Romans 8:37
- Ephesians 2:10
- Colossians 3:12
- Matthew 5:13-16
- Psalm 32:9

Books and Commentaries on Nehemiah:

- Kidner, Derek. *Ezra and Nehemiah: An Introduction and Commentary.* InterVarsity Press, 1979.
- Yamauchi, Edwin M. *Expositor's Bible Commentary: Ezra, Nehemiah, Esther.* Zondervan, 1988.
- Breneman, Mervin. *The New American Commentary: Ezra, Nehemiah, Esther.* B&H Publishing, 1993.

Books on Restoration and Christian Living:

- Tozer, A.W. *The Pursuit of God.* Christian Publications, 1948.

- Lewis, C.S. *Mere Christianity.* HarperOne, 1952.

- Meyer, Joyce. *Battlefield of the Mind: Winning the Battle in Your Mind.* FaithWords, 1995.

Additional Sources of Inspiration:

- Spurgeon, Charles H. *Morning and Evening Devotionals.* Fleming H. Revell Company, 1866.

- T.D. Jakes. *Crushing: God Turns Pressure into Power.* FaithWords, 2019.

Online References and Sermons:

- Blue Letter Bible (www.blueletterbible.org)

- Bible Gateway (www.biblegateway.com)

- Various teachings and sermons from NDM (New Destiny Ministry)

This bibliography reflects the sources and inspirations that have contributed to the writing of *Rise Up and Build, My Time of Restoration*, guiding its message of spiritual renewal, perseverance, and the faith-driven journey toward restoration.

About The Author

Stephen Irie is a Spiritual Leader, writer, artist, business man, and publisher who has dedicated his life to inspiring and empowering others. As the founder and president of the New Destiny Ministry and CEO of Iries Publishing, he has built a platform that combines his passions for faith, education, and personal development.

In 1999, during a transformative period of dry fasting — 40 days and 40 nights — Stephen experienced a life-changing encounter with the Holy Spirit that marked the beginning of a profound spiritual journey. During this time, he received the message of "**Mankind's Identity**," which would become the central theme of his work.

From that moment on, Stephen dedicated himself to sharing the powerful message of identity, helping others discover their true selves in alignment with God's purpose.

Resident in London, UK, Stephen holds a Master of Divinity (M.Div.), a Bachelor of Arts (Honors) in Business Accounting and Finance, and a Postgraduate Certificate in Education (PGCE QTS).

His diverse academic background, combined with his deep faith and experience in leadership, equips him to serve a wide audience, offering guidance on personal growth, professional success, and spiritual renewal.

Through his ministry, Stephen continues to inspire individuals to rise up, embrace their identity, and walk in their God-given purpose. His work with New Destiny Ministry and Iries Publishing is a testament to his unwavering commitment to helping people achieve lasting transformation in all areas of life.

For enquiries, speaking engagements, partnership or any form of communication, please contact us through the following media:

stephenirie@hotmail.com,
+44 (0)7925525434

OracleIrie @ Facebook/ Meta, Instagram, X, TikTok...
www.stephenirie.com

About The Publisher

The Iries Publishing is a London-based publishing house with over many years of experience in the publishing industry. Dedicated to helping authors bring their visions to life, The Iries Publishing has proudly published dozens of books across various genres, offering readers quality content that inspires, informs, and captivates.

With a reputation for excellence and a passion for storytelling, The Iries Publishing works closely with authors to ensure their messages reach global audiences. From concept to print, the company focuses on creating impactful books that leave a lasting legacy.

For inquiries or collaboration opportunities, feel free to contact us:

stephenirie@hotmail.com,
+44 (0)7925525434

OracleIrie @ Facebook/ Meta, Instagram, X, TikTok…
www.stephenirie.com

Let **The Iries Publishing** help you share your story with the world.

www.ingramcontent.com/pod-product-compliance
Lightning Source LLC
Chambersburg PA
CBHW070511090426
42735CB00012B/2733